FX TRADING | MAKE MONEY ONLINE

TRADING FOREX WITH OTHER PEOPLE'S MONEY

Paul Ardennes

2021 ULTIMATE FINANCING FOR FOREX TRADERS | XMAS PRESENT

MAKE MONEY ONLINE OR GIFT AS A PANDEMIC PRESENT TO THOSE LOVED ONES WHO NEED A NEW DIRECTION IN THEIR LIFE | NEW COURSE

PAUL ARDENNES

This book was published thanks to free support and training from:

The Wall Street Investors' Club

CONTENTS

INTRODUCTION

I came into trading by chance. I was researching some material for one of my Amazon ebooks on transcendental energies when I stumbled upon some forex competitions that attracted my attention. What is forex and how people win money on competitions? These were my immediate questions. After a few mishaps, I kind of reversed-engineered the various systems on offer online. I came up with some algorithmic trading strategies that could be handled to become consistent in their results. After some practice, I jumped into the competition registrations. A couple of months went by and some 20 competitions passed along.

Pretty soon after having tweaked my robots, I was able to get somewhere, and I mean on the top 20 positions. I needed some form of calculator to beat the best traders there and not get too much behind the rest. I designed my own professional calculator after many trials and errors. Then I took 6th place. After a couple more months, I managed to take 1st, 2nd, 3d, 4th ,5th and 6th place in the same competition consecutively. No need to say that the first 3 positions were enough to get good money. I thought that winning competitions might lead to bigger things if I could get capital high enough to make sense of trading. I did a deep research on funding institutions and this course was drafted. I then wrote a Udemy course from it. The rest is past, gone and background that I dusted.

Udemy Course Description

This course takes you into the finding of a research that I did when I was winning competitions. As I was winning real money, it came to my mind that perhaps there were institutions out there that could be interested in my trading results. After extensive research, I made a list of all funding institutions that I could talk to. The ones that I shortlisted are listed below to save you a bit of research. I joined a few to get a good funding portfolio and a diversity of strategies deployed over this portfolio. If you need some trading strategies, have a look at my other courses and books.

Happy Pips

PRELUDE ON FUNDING

There is a shift of thinking in the world of financial institutions in Wall Street and around the world.

It used to be the case where big offices and vast reward schemes, wild parties and extravagant clients' diners were big times and customary.

Recessions after recessions and markets crashes created the shift. Now, trading institutions prefer finding and funding retail traders, who work from home. As long as you are efficient and consistent, the money is there waiting for you to catch.

The clever bit that I found from the beginning is that the funding institutions will give a chance to almost anyone as long as we cover our risk to them.

I was in a position to understand their positioning on that. If I was to risk let's say 4% of their capital of $10000, that would be $400 gone. So, it would make sense for them to let me have their capital of $10K if I was prepared to let them have at least $400 to cover their losses. But that would just cover the drawdown, the risk of trading. It would not cover their biggest loss, the loss of interest on their capital had they left it invested. That usually is in the region of 6% on a small capital of $10K. So, the cleverness of this guys was to protect both losses by asking the retail trader for $1000 to cover it all. I thought that this was genius of them. I created a small earning calculator and found out that in any circumstances, I would still be making 4 times more revenue on positive trading if I was funded than if I was using my own $1000 with a broker. Now, my next job was to find a reputable institution where I could drop my $1000 and get a live funded account of $10K. That happened pretty quickly. I even got 5% discount for asking. The very happy me now had a "LIVE" account written on my trading platform on the next morning.

Hopefully, you can make good use of this research. I teach the fundamentals in a Udemy course. I am funded by the Wall Street Investors' Club, an exclusive private club that only accepts new members by private introduction from their members. As a member, I am glad to give you this opportunity to join if this is your choice. (You will find the password for the website in the resources of the course). If not, I am introducing many other institutions that you may test as you wish. The secret is to join a few to diversify your live accounts.

FORMAT OF LISTINGS

I will try to keep consistency in listing the institutions where you can get funding for your forex trading goals. You need to do your own due diligence once you gain knowledge of their existence. They can be found on the internet if you do some profound research. I am putting some of them in one place.

To do that, I will use the following systematology:

Name of institution

Website

Promo video (if available)

Rules/parameters

Costs of participation

My views and comments

TRADENET

https://www.tradenet.com/trading-challenge/

Promo video

Rules/parameters

We get a trading account of $14K once the challenge is passed. The challenge funding itself is of $10K.

It mentions a DD daily of $100 and maximum DD of $300. Exceeding these closes automatically the challenge.

This challenge seems to be asking a 3 days out of 5 trading days to be active.

All positions must be closed by the end of the trading day. I assume that they use GMT.

It looks like we need to provide a profit of $500 out of a capital of $14000 funded by this institution, in a week (5 trading days).

A minimum of 6 orders must be placed per day and a maximum of 20.

Profits of at least $100 per day on at least 2 days out of the five.

Costs of participation $0.00

My views and comments

Trying to make sense of all this, algorithmic trading would probably not be suitable. With algorithmic trading, it is hard to control when a robot decides to take on a trade. We probably would not be able to provide the minimum of 6 trades even if we had 20 robots running at the same time. Furthermore, we would not be able to control the risk level of the combined open orders since we would not know how many robots would fire on during the day.

Trading the news release would not be suitable because that would only be one or two trade during the day. They want 6 minimum.

It looks like the only viable solution is a manual trading strategy like randomness. Just open 6 charts instead of the 8 suggested in the course in Udemy on randomness. That's your 6 trades for the day. You need to start early morning since all trades must be closed by end of trading day to respect that rule.

With a challenge capital of $10K, we need to trade a number of lots so that the daily risk is $16 per trade ($16*6= $96). That is 0.16% Risk on capital per trade. That represents 0.05 lot per currency for a 30 pips SL. We would need to set our TP>30 to get a RRR of better than 1:1. In fact, I always avoid to use a TP (Take Profit level). Instead, I use an exit robot to close all orders when the equity is at my defined and specified target. Et voilà, the formula is setup for the challenge.

Make good use of the calculator on the website https://wallstreetinvestors.club to get your lots right.

<u>Views that I may find from Forums or their own users.</u>

Reviews seem to point to failures caused by lack of understanding of the rules. But you know better. If you have studied my other courses, you know how to use efficiently and accurately a calculator to place your stop loss and to calculate your number of lots that represent your risk level.

WALL STREET INVESTORS' CLUB

Website: https:wallstreetinvestors.club

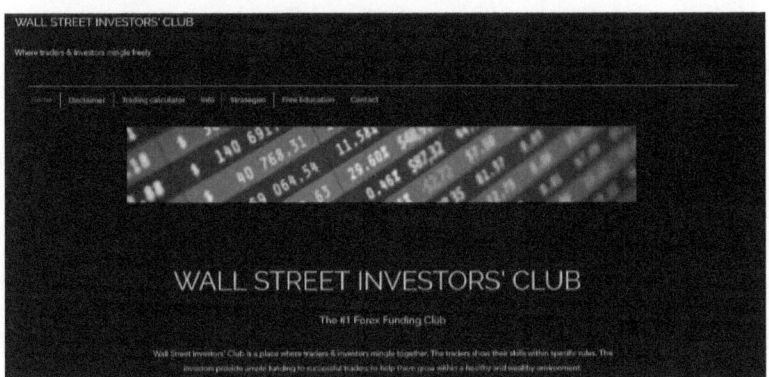

Rules/parameters

Drawdown maximum at any time 4%

Funded Capital: $10K per yearly membership (you get every year $10K funds on renewal of your membership) – Capital increase of 100% per 10% gain

Costs of participation: It is a yearly membership to the private club. It is at the moment $1K

0.5 lot maximum per $10K funding. There is a 40% profit sharing. The investors keep 60%.

Full rules are provided on enrollment.

My views and comments

I chose this club because of the yearly membership, the participation in course creation and the calculator online that makes things easier and is not accessible to non-members since the website is password protected. The club has interesting trading applications like EA studio and real-time news trading app available directly from the website. Also, I find it easy to program and follow the rules of trading. The added benefit of joining this club is the doubling of the capital every time a 10% profit is achieved. I use neural network artificial intelligence combined into an excel add-in that I had designed for my predictive inputs. I am preparing a course on the subject. Look for the announcement from Udemy.

The password to the website changes every 2 weeks and is available in the resources of the Udemy course.

TOPSTEPFX

Website: https://www.topstepfx.com/

Rules/parameters

They work in 2 steps

Step 1 requires a profit of $3000 (1% of capital), a risk of $2K with a maximum of 3 lots. If we take the EURUSD as an example and a SL of 50 pips, the parameters are based on 0.5% risk @ $1500 for all open orders. See calculator on website. This will vary with the SL size and the currency traded.

All positions have to be closed on market close on Fridays.

Step 2 lowers the risk for their weekly loss limit to $1K instead of $2K. It adds the extra rule of not trading during economic news releases impacting the currency traded. That means that any currency with an open order running that will be in the news listed on their agreement needs to be closed at least one minute before the news are released. We can trade any other currency not in the news.

Costs of participation

There are several choices. I've selected the **$300K Buying Power** for this explanation. But you can have a look at their website and decide what is best for you if you choose them to fund you.

The cost for this selection is $165/month for 3K capital*

My views and comments

I try not to participate to schemes of funding that restrict trading during news (my best sessions) or force a closing of trades during weekends. Since I use algorithmic trading, these restrictions are limiting too much and would need special programming inbuilt into the robots. The drawdown seems very low on first hand but the leverage is 1:100.

Also, the cost involved is quite high at $165/month ($1980/year). *It must be remembered that a $300K _Buying Power_ really means $3K in real terms on a 1:100 leverage. The monthly fee seems to be permanent until we decide to have our account closed or the rules are broken and they withdraw funding.

As a business model, I can understand their structure. They charge a monthly fee to everyone and fund the few who manage to prove that they can trade successfully with the monthly fees of those who can't make it plus the monthly fees of those who can make it. It's a win/win system.

The 5ers.

*Please note that the 5ers have kindly provided **10% discount** to our students on any scheme you enroll in **until the end of this month**. Just use the link above in this ebook, on the website or in the Udemy course.* (The offer is not available anywhere else) – You pay the full price and then they refund you the 10%. They don't have an automatized system since they don't do this offer to outsiders.

Although the best value on offer is the $40000 ($10K during the trial), I suggest that you choose the cheapest package to start with to see how it feels to have a "Live" account on MT4

Rules/parameters

This funding institution has simple rules easy to understand. The DD is 4%. The profit at first is 6%. Once this is reached, the funding is automatic. For every 10% gain, the account is doubled. The maximum risk in lots is 0.5 for the $10K account. The rules are easily implemented in a calculator. The cost of $400 is a one off fee and is reasonable. I understand that there is no training, just an email support. Once the 6% trial gain is achieved, the account jumps to $40K.

Costs of participation varies.

$ 52,000 Funded fx Account	$ 40,000 Funded fx Account	$ 24,000 Funded fx Account
Trade a $13,000 Live Account to Qualify	Trade a $10,000 Live Account to Qualify	Trade a $6,000 Live Account to Qualify
$550 Once-off Fee	$400 Once-off Fee	$270 Once-off Fee
Target $910	Target $600	Target $375
Drawdown $520	Drawdown $400	Drawdown $250
Max. Exposure 0.65 Lot	Max. Exposure 0.50 Lot	Max. Exposure 0.30 Lot
Profit Share 50%	Profit Share 50%	Profit Share 50%
Double Growth for 10%	Double Growth for 10%	Double Growth for 10%
Enroll	Enroll	Enroll

See diagram above. Just divide by 4 the funding account to find out the funds provided during trial. (E.g. a $40K Live funded account is $10K Live during the trial period until you manage 6% gain. As soon as this is achieved, your MT4 platform will show $40K Live the next morning.

My views and comments

Because I understand the trading rules, I like this setup plus the generous discount to my Students. It is one of the funders in my portfolio of funding institutions that I have joined so far. I guess that 10% is achievable within a month or two but they don't have a time restriction. So I can see a capital growth substantial enough within a year or two. With $40K, we can trade 2 full lots. That's 2.5% risk on a 50 pips SL on the EURUSD (as an example to illustrate). There is a 50% profit sharing. There is a calculator especially designed for this on the Wall Street website.

Capital	10000		
Total # of trades	8	Total allowance	0.5
Maximum lots per trade	0.063		

You only need to input your capital as indicated on the MT4 platform and the number of trades you are going to order.

SAVIUS LLC

Website: http://www.saviusllc.com/become-a-savius-trader-2/

Rules/parameters

There are 3 phases in this funding scheme

Phase 1. The trader takes the challenge and trades for 10 consecutive days (2 weeks). Maximum DD $1500 and daily drawdown $750 for a capital of $20000

To qualify for phase 2, the target is $2K. If the trader passes phase 1, the participation fee is refunded.

Phase 2 continues on simulation and lasts for 30 days. The profit target is $3K and the total DD is $2K.

Phase 3: live and simulation funding.

Costs of participation $198

My views and comments

The daily DD is a bit less than I'm used to but the maximum DD is more generous. My funders normally ask for 4%.

You can choose 1 of 2 paths. The path 1 is for experienced traders who do not require any training. They trade their own strategies. Path 2 is for those who need training. It's called the Junior Savius trader path.

The challenge is mandatory and is to assess the capabilities of the trader. I can see myself failing to follow some rules as there are plenty and varied.

FTMO

Website https://ftmo.com/en/welcome/

Rules/parameters

You start with a 30 days challenge on a simulated account (demo). This is the tough time in their scheme. The TP is set at 10%. The daily DD is 5% and max DD is 10%. 50% of your trading days have to be positive. If you achieve the target in 10 days (the minimum) instead of 30, you must have at least 5 days with positive results. It's one of these rules where I'm not sure of the purpose. Perhaps it shows consistency in trading. You can't trade in less than 10days.

Once you pass the challenge, you go through a second round of testing called a verification process. In this phase, they double the number of days to 60 days and lower your TP by half (5%). This becomes a much better proposition. I wish they could make the challenge with these rules.

Once both tests are passed in accordance with the rules being respected, you become an FTMO trader. Your account still shows "Demo" but in fact, your demo account is now connected to a live account in their trading room. There is a 70% profit sharing.

Costs of participation

€155 for $10000 (notice the 2 currencies)

My views and comments

I like the concept but I don't like the time restriction. I tried their funding 3 times and because of this time restriction, I failed every time. What I like is that if we remain in profit, they give us a new challenge for free. I had a few of them but somehow I don't manage to reach the profit target on time. So I opened a few accounts with the 5ers instead. They are more expensive to join but the lack of time restriction makes for it since the capital doubles at every 10% gain, whatever the time it takes to reach it.

They use the following brokers for their feeds

And they have MT4, MT5 or cTrader as trading platforms.

EARN 2 TRADE

https://www.earn2trade.com/gauntlet-mini

Rules/parameters

They offer a choice of capital. We'll study the $25K here. It seems that there is no time limit for the evaluation although they mention 15 days at least. I assume that the minimum is 15 days and there is no maximum to achieve the target.

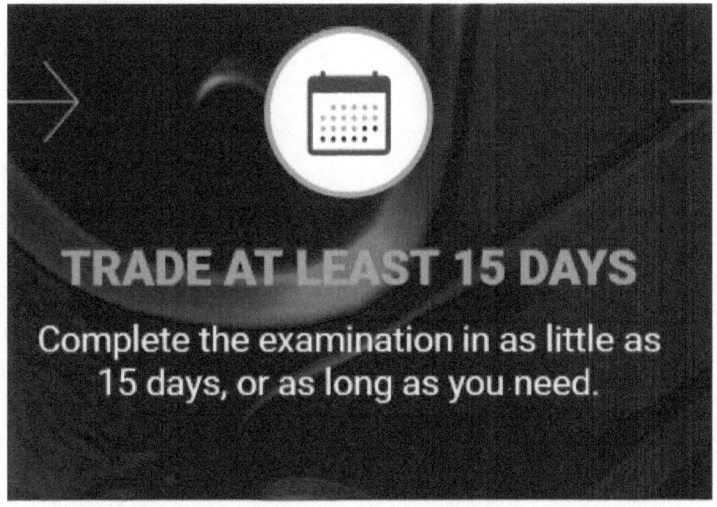

TRADE AT LEAST 15 DAYS

Complete the examination in as little as 15 days, or as long as you need.

It looks like we need to pay $125 after 90 days to access their trading platform. And $78 to access their journal facility. I can't see whether these amounts are charged monthly or on a one-off basis. Again, I assume that this is monthly.

On up to $1500 profit, we can trade 2 contracts. Above $1500, we can trade 3 contracts.

Costs of participation

For the $25K, it costs $150 per month. There is a fee of $40 per month for access to the data.

My views and comments

I'll pass on this opportunity. It's not for me. First, I don't particularly like monthly fees and second, there are too many "other" costs. Good luck if you choose them. Let me know how it goes.

CONCLUSION

I reviewed 23 financial institutions that provide funding to retail traders. Only a handful passed my criteria of choice. Hopefully, you found a funding institution that took you over. If you are still not ready for investing $1000 in your future, take this time to practice, simulate and learn the ropes to success. I personally work with the Wall Street investors' club and the 5ers. I am still looking at the other opportunities as they appear online. I tried FTMO without success. I like to be funded by at least 5 institutions. For this, I reinvest the profits from the others all the time. That builds up a decent capital to trade with and enables to vary the strategies.

There is room for everyone in forex trading. Whether you decide to trade the Economic News Release, or use algorithmic trading (let the robots do it) or perhaps trading with indicators or mix them up, there is some pleasure in mastering the skills and putting them in live real-time context.

You can do it. Do it.

ABOUT THE AUTHOR

"Paul Ardennes is an Author. He is working with various publishers including *Amazon* and *Barnes & Noble*.

He publishes courses on educational platforms such as *Udemy* & *Simpliv* on **Spiritual Yoga and Forex trading**.

He is a trained Electronic Medicine practitioner (Scenar Cosmodic, Auricular therapy, Acupoints charting, electronic iris analysis, laser therapy and so on...), **an energy healer** (Seichim and Usui Reiki Master, informational medicine) **and a Forex researcher** (Algorithmic trading, fundamentals and technical fx trading).

He was introduced to Forex while researching yet another book. To cut a short story shorter, he got involved in forex competitions and started winning them and collecting money prizes.

That is when he discovered *Wall Street Investors' Club*, a private club where you enter by personal invitation only. They funded his trading skills.

His goal is to **impart stillness and silentness** within the emotional, turmoiled and turbulent minds of societies. He founded ***Spiritual Yoga*** to help with this ambition. Whether you join him to trade Forex for a second income or join him in the quest to inward peace and calm, the choice is there either way.

He is married to a Doctor gynaecologist and has 1 indigo son. They all live in Central America.

Join the parties. Join the Clubs"

Amazon Editorial Vine Team Member

COURSES BY PAUL ARDENNES

Prices may vary

Algorithmic trading |
communiqués de presse...

Paul Ardennes

★ ★ ★ ★ 2.9 (4)

£199.99 £11.99

Forex Trading|
Algorithmic trading | W...

Paul Ardennes

★ ★ ★ ★ 3.5 (10)

£199.99 £11.99

London Open | Trade what
bankers trade every...

Paul Ardennes

★ ★ ★ ★ 3.1 (17)

£199.99 £11.99

Using Randomness to
trade FX Currency pairs ...

Paul Ardennes

★ ★ ★ ★ 3.1 (12)

£199.99 £11.99

News release trading | FX
Trading | Forex | Online...

Paul Ardennes

★ ★ ★ ★ 3.6 (11)

£199.99 £11.99